50 Easy-to-Make Sweets for Beginners

By: Kelly Johnson

Table of Contents

- Chocolate Dipped Strawberries
- Rice Krispies Treats
- No-Bake Cheesecake Bites
- Sugar Cookies
- Chocolate Truffles
- Chocolate Covered Pretzels
- Apple Slices with Caramel
- Brownie Bites
- Fruit Salad with Honey Drizzle
- Peanut Butter Chocolate Bars
- Vanilla Cupcakes
- Oreo Truffles
- Cinnamon Sugar Tortilla Chips
- Marshmallow Treats
- Lemon Bars
- Chocolate Bark with Nuts and Dried Fruit
- Simple Chocolate Fudge
- Cookie Dough Bites
- Chocolate Pudding
- Nutella Stuffed Crescent Rolls
- Banana Bread
- Rice Pudding
- Homemade Chocolate Chip Cookies
- Shortbread Cookies
- Caramelized Banana Slices
- Mini Eclairs
- Panna Cotta
- S'mores Bars
- Frozen Yogurt Bark
- Almond Joy Bites
- Apple Nachos
- Chocolate Covered Bananas
- Coconut Macaroons
- Strawberry Sorbet
- Churros

- Key Lime Pie Bites
- Fruit Popsicles
- Brownie Cookies
- Mini Cheesecakes
- Snickerdoodle Cookies
- Chocolate Lava Mug Cake
- Chocolate Peanut Butter Cups
- Pumpkin Spice Muffins
- Lemon Sorbet
- No-Bake Oatmeal Cookies
- White Chocolate Raspberry Bark
- Simple Ice Cream Sandwiches
- Chocolate Coconut Energy Balls
- Pineapple Coconut Bites
- Jello Parfaits

Chocolate Dipped Strawberries

Ingredients:

- 1 lb fresh strawberries, washed and dried
- 8 oz dark or milk chocolate, chopped
- 4 oz white chocolate (optional, for drizzling)

Instructions:

1. Line a baking sheet with parchment paper.
2. In a heatproof bowl, melt the dark or milk chocolate over a double boiler or in the microwave in 30-second intervals, stirring until smooth.
3. Hold each strawberry by the stem and dip it into the melted chocolate, coating about two-thirds of the strawberry. Let excess chocolate drip off.
4. Place the dipped strawberries on the prepared baking sheet.
5. If using white chocolate, melt it and drizzle over the dipped strawberries for decoration.
6. Let the chocolate set at room temperature or refrigerate for 15 minutes.

Rice Krispies Treats

Ingredients:

- 3 tbsp unsalted butter
- 1 package (10 oz) mini marshmallows
- 6 cups Rice Krispies cereal

Instructions:

1. Melt the butter in a large saucepan over low heat.
2. Add the marshmallows and stir until melted and smooth.
3. Remove from heat and add the Rice Krispies cereal, stirring until evenly coated.
4. Pour the mixture into a greased 9x13-inch pan and press it down with a spatula to form an even layer.
5. Let the treats cool and set for about 30 minutes before cutting into squares.

No-Bake Cheesecake Bites

Ingredients:

- 8 oz cream cheese, softened
- 1/2 cup powdered sugar
- 1 tsp vanilla extract
- 1 cup graham cracker crumbs
- 1/4 cup melted butter
- 1/4 cup fruit preserves or fresh fruit (optional)

Instructions:

1. In a mixing bowl, beat together the cream cheese, powdered sugar, and vanilla extract until smooth.
2. In another bowl, mix the graham cracker crumbs with melted butter.
3. Shape the cream cheese mixture into small balls and then roll them in the graham cracker crumbs to coat.
4. If desired, top each bite with a spoonful of fruit preserves or fresh fruit.
5. Refrigerate for 30 minutes before serving.

Sugar Cookies

Ingredients:

- 2 3/4 cups all-purpose flour
- 1 tsp baking soda
- 1/2 tsp baking powder
- 1 cup unsalted butter, softened
- 1 1/2 cups granulated sugar
- 1 egg
- 1 tsp vanilla extract
- 1/2 tsp almond extract (optional)
- 1/4 cup sugar for rolling

Instructions:

1. Preheat oven to 375°F (190°C). Line a baking sheet with parchment paper.
2. In a bowl, whisk together flour, baking soda, and baking powder.
3. In another bowl, beat the butter and granulated sugar together until creamy. Add the egg, vanilla extract, and almond extract (if using).
4. Gradually add the dry ingredients to the wet ingredients, mixing until combined.
5. Roll dough into 1-inch balls and then roll in sugar. Place on the prepared baking sheet and flatten slightly with a fork.
6. Bake for 8-10 minutes, or until edges are golden. Let cool on a wire rack.

Chocolate Truffles

Ingredients:

- 8 oz dark or milk chocolate, chopped
- 1/2 cup heavy cream
- 1 tsp vanilla extract
- Cocoa powder, chopped nuts, or sprinkles (for coating)

Instructions:

1. Heat the heavy cream in a small saucepan over medium heat until it begins to simmer.
2. Pour the hot cream over the chopped chocolate and let sit for a few minutes before stirring until smooth.
3. Stir in vanilla extract and refrigerate the mixture for about 1-2 hours until firm enough to scoop.
4. Use a spoon or melon baller to form small balls of the chocolate mixture. Roll each truffle in cocoa powder, chopped nuts, or sprinkles.
5. Refrigerate until firm and serve.

Chocolate Covered Pretzels

Ingredients:

- 1 bag of mini pretzels
- 8 oz dark or milk chocolate, melted
- Sprinkles, crushed candy, or sea salt (optional)

Instructions:

1. Line a baking sheet with parchment paper.
2. Dip each pretzel halfway into the melted chocolate and place on the prepared baking sheet.
3. Sprinkle with toppings such as sprinkles, crushed candy, or a pinch of sea salt, if desired.
4. Let the chocolate set at room temperature or refrigerate for 10-15 minutes until firm.

Apple Slices with Caramel

Ingredients:

- 4 apples, sliced
- 1 cup caramel sauce (store-bought or homemade)
- Chopped nuts (optional)

Instructions:

1. Slice the apples into wedges and arrange them on a serving platter.
2. Warm the caramel sauce slightly if needed and drizzle over the apple slices.
3. Top with chopped nuts for added crunch if desired. Serve immediately.

Brownie Bites

Ingredients:

- 1 box of brownie mix (or homemade brownie batter)
- 1/4 cup vegetable oil
- 2 large eggs
- 1/2 tsp vanilla extract
- Mini chocolate chips (optional)

Instructions:

1. Preheat oven to 350°F (175°C). Grease or line a mini muffin tin with paper liners.
2. Prepare brownie batter according to package instructions, adding the eggs, oil, and vanilla extract.
3. Scoop batter into the mini muffin tin, filling each cup about halfway. Optionally, add mini chocolate chips on top.
4. Bake for 10-12 minutes, or until a toothpick comes out with just a few crumbs. Let cool before serving.

Fruit Salad with Honey Drizzle

Ingredients:

- 2 cups strawberries, hulled and sliced
- 2 cups pineapple, cubed
- 1 cup blueberries
- 1 cup grapes, halved
- 1 orange, peeled and cut into segments
- 2 tbsp honey
- 1 tbsp fresh lemon juice
- 1/2 tsp vanilla extract (optional)

Instructions:

1. In a large mixing bowl, combine all the prepared fruit.
2. In a small bowl, whisk together the honey, lemon juice, and vanilla extract (if using).
3. Drizzle the honey mixture over the fruit and toss gently to combine.
4. Serve immediately or refrigerate for 30 minutes before serving for a chilled option.

Peanut Butter Chocolate Bars

Ingredients:

- 1 cup peanut butter
- 1/2 cup butter, melted
- 2 cups powdered sugar
- 1 1/2 cups graham cracker crumbs
- 1 cup chocolate chips
- 1 tbsp vegetable oil

Instructions:

1. In a large bowl, mix together peanut butter, melted butter, powdered sugar, and graham cracker crumbs until well combined.
2. Press the mixture into the bottom of a greased 9x13-inch baking dish.
3. In a microwave-safe bowl, melt the chocolate chips with vegetable oil in 30-second intervals, stirring until smooth.
4. Pour the melted chocolate over the peanut butter layer and spread it evenly.
5. Refrigerate for at least 2 hours before cutting into bars and serving.

Vanilla Cupcakes

Ingredients:

- 1 1/2 cups all-purpose flour
- 1 1/2 tsp baking powder
- 1/4 tsp salt
- 1/2 cup unsalted butter, softened
- 3/4 cup granulated sugar
- 2 large eggs
- 1 tsp vanilla extract
- 1/2 cup milk

Instructions:

1. Preheat the oven to 350°F (175°C) and line a muffin tin with paper liners.
2. In a medium bowl, whisk together the flour, baking powder, and salt.
3. In a large bowl, beat together the butter and sugar until light and fluffy. Add the eggs one at a time, beating well after each addition, then add the vanilla extract.
4. Gradually add the dry ingredients to the wet ingredients, alternating with the milk, beginning and ending with the dry ingredients.
5. Divide the batter evenly among the cupcake liners, filling each about two-thirds full.
6. Bake for 18-20 minutes, or until a toothpick inserted into the center comes out clean. Let cool completely before frosting.

Oreo Truffles

Ingredients:

- 1 package (14 oz) Oreo cookies
- 8 oz cream cheese, softened
- 8 oz chocolate (dark or milk), melted

Instructions:

1. Crush the Oreo cookies into fine crumbs using a food processor or by placing them in a plastic bag and crushing with a rolling pin.
2. In a large bowl, combine the Oreo crumbs with the softened cream cheese, mixing until smooth.
3. Roll the mixture into 1-inch balls and place them on a baking sheet lined with parchment paper.
4. Dip each ball into the melted chocolate, coating evenly, and return to the baking sheet.
5. Refrigerate for at least 30 minutes until set before serving.

Cinnamon Sugar Tortilla Chips

Ingredients:

- 4 flour tortillas
- 1/4 cup unsalted butter, melted
- 1/4 cup granulated sugar
- 1 tsp ground cinnamon

Instructions:

1. Preheat the oven to 350°F (175°C) and line a baking sheet with parchment paper.
2. Cut the tortillas into triangles (like slices of a pizza) and arrange them in a single layer on the baking sheet.
3. Brush the tortilla triangles with melted butter and sprinkle with a mixture of sugar and cinnamon.
4. Bake for 10-12 minutes or until golden and crispy. Let cool before serving.

Marshmallow Treats

Ingredients:

- 4 cups mini marshmallows
- 3 tbsp unsalted butter
- 6 cups Rice Krispies cereal

Instructions:

1. In a large saucepan, melt the butter over low heat. Add the marshmallows and stir until completely melted and smooth.
2. Remove from heat and stir in the Rice Krispies cereal until evenly coated.
3. Press the mixture into a greased 9x13-inch baking dish and let it cool for about 30 minutes before cutting into squares.

Lemon Bars

Ingredients:

- **For the crust:**
    - 1 1/2 cups all-purpose flour
    - 1/4 cup powdered sugar
    - 1/2 cup unsalted butter, softened
- **For the filling:**
    - 2 large eggs
    - 1 cup granulated sugar
    - 1/4 cup all-purpose flour
    - 1/4 tsp baking powder
    - 1/2 cup fresh lemon juice
    - Powdered sugar for dusting

Instructions:

1. Preheat the oven to 350°F (175°C). Grease a 9x9-inch baking dish.
2. For the crust: In a bowl, combine the flour, powdered sugar, and softened butter. Mix until the dough forms. Press the dough into the prepared baking dish to form the crust.
3. Bake the crust for 15-20 minutes, or until slightly golden.
4. For the filling: In a bowl, whisk together the eggs, granulated sugar, flour, baking powder, and lemon juice. Pour over the baked crust.
5. Bake for an additional 20-25 minutes, or until the filling is set.
6. Let cool, then dust with powdered sugar and cut into squares.

Chocolate Bark with Nuts and Dried Fruit

Ingredients:

- 8 oz dark or milk chocolate, chopped
- 1/2 cup mixed nuts (almonds, walnuts, pecans), chopped
- 1/2 cup dried fruit (cranberries, raisins, apricots), chopped

Instructions:

1. Line a baking sheet with parchment paper.
2. Melt the chocolate in a heatproof bowl over a double boiler or in the microwave, stirring until smooth.
3. Pour the melted chocolate onto the prepared baking sheet and spread into an even layer.
4. Sprinkle the chopped nuts and dried fruit over the chocolate, pressing gently to adhere.
5. Refrigerate for 1-2 hours until the chocolate is set. Break into pieces and serve.

Simple Chocolate Fudge

Ingredients:

- 2 cups semi-sweet chocolate chips
- 1 can (14 oz) sweetened condensed milk
- 1/4 cup unsalted butter
- 1 tsp vanilla extract

Instructions:

1. Line an 8x8-inch baking pan with parchment paper.
2. In a saucepan, combine the chocolate chips, sweetened condensed milk, and butter over low heat.
3. Stir constantly until the chocolate chips are melted and the mixture is smooth.
4. Remove from heat and stir in the vanilla extract.
5. Pour the mixture into the prepared pan and spread it evenly.
6. Refrigerate for at least 2 hours until firm. Cut into squares and serve.

Cookie Dough Bites

Ingredients:

- 1/2 cup unsalted butter, softened
- 1/2 cup brown sugar
- 1/4 cup granulated sugar
- 1 tsp vanilla extract
- 1 cup all-purpose flour (heat-treated for safety)
- 1/4 tsp salt
- 1/3 cup mini chocolate chips
- 2 tbsp milk

Instructions:

1. In a bowl, beat the butter, brown sugar, and granulated sugar until light and fluffy.
2. Add the vanilla extract, and mix in the flour and salt. Stir until fully combined.
3. Add milk a tablespoon at a time until the dough reaches a thick but scoopable consistency.
4. Fold in the mini chocolate chips.
5. Roll the dough into small bite-sized balls and place them on a baking sheet lined with parchment paper.
6. Refrigerate for 1-2 hours before serving.

Chocolate Pudding

Ingredients:

- 2 3/4 cups whole milk
- 1/2 cup granulated sugar
- 1/4 cup unsweetened cocoa powder
- 1/4 cup cornstarch
- 1/8 tsp salt
- 3 large egg yolks
- 2 tbsp unsalted butter
- 1 tsp vanilla extract

Instructions:

1. In a medium saucepan, whisk together the milk, sugar, cocoa powder, cornstarch, and salt over medium heat.
2. In a separate bowl, whisk the egg yolks.
3. Gradually add the egg yolks to the milk mixture while whisking constantly.
4. Continue cooking the mixture, whisking frequently, until it thickens and comes to a boil.
5. Once thickened, remove from heat and stir in the butter and vanilla extract.
6. Pour the pudding into serving bowls and refrigerate for 2 hours before serving.

Nutella Stuffed Crescent Rolls

Ingredients:

- 1 can (8 oz) crescent roll dough
- 1/2 cup Nutella
- Powdered sugar for dusting (optional)

Instructions:

1. Preheat the oven to 375°F (190°C) and line a baking sheet with parchment paper.
2. Unroll the crescent dough and separate into individual triangles.
3. Place about 1 tablespoon of Nutella at the wide end of each triangle.
4. Roll the dough up starting from the wide end, enclosing the Nutella inside.
5. Bake for 10-12 minutes or until golden brown.
6. Dust with powdered sugar before serving, if desired.

Banana Bread

Ingredients:

- 1 1/2 cups all-purpose flour
- 1 tsp baking soda
- 1/4 tsp salt
- 1/2 cup unsalted butter, softened
- 3/4 cup granulated sugar
- 2 large eggs
- 4 ripe bananas, mashed
- 1 tsp vanilla extract
- 1/2 cup sour cream or yogurt

Instructions:

1. Preheat the oven to 350°F (175°C). Grease and flour a loaf pan.
2. In a bowl, mix the flour, baking soda, and salt.
3. In another large bowl, beat the butter and sugar together until creamy. Add the eggs one at a time, beating well after each addition.
4. Stir in the mashed bananas and vanilla extract.
5. Add the flour mixture and sour cream alternately, beginning and ending with the flour mixture.
6. Pour the batter into the prepared pan and bake for 60-70 minutes, or until a toothpick inserted into the center comes out clean.
7. Let the bread cool in the pan for 10 minutes before transferring to a wire rack.

Rice Pudding

Ingredients:

- 1/2 cup short-grain white rice
- 2 1/2 cups whole milk
- 1/2 cup granulated sugar
- 1/4 tsp salt
- 1 tsp vanilla extract
- 1/2 tsp ground cinnamon (optional)

Instructions:

1. In a medium saucepan, combine the rice, milk, sugar, and salt. Bring to a simmer over medium heat.
2. Reduce the heat to low and cook, stirring occasionally, for 20-25 minutes, or until the rice is tender and the pudding thickens.
3. Remove from heat and stir in the vanilla extract.
4. Let the pudding cool slightly before serving, and top with cinnamon if desired.

Homemade Chocolate Chip Cookies

Ingredients:

- 2 1/4 cups all-purpose flour
- 1/2 tsp baking soda
- 1 cup unsalted butter, softened
- 1/2 cup granulated sugar
- 1 cup packed brown sugar
- 1 tsp vanilla extract
- 2 large eggs
- 2 cups semi-sweet chocolate chips
- 1/2 tsp salt

Instructions:

1. Preheat the oven to 350°F (175°C) and line baking sheets with parchment paper.
2. In a bowl, whisk together the flour, baking soda, and salt.
3. In a large bowl, beat the butter, granulated sugar, brown sugar, and vanilla extract until creamy.
4. Add the eggs one at a time, beating well after each addition.
5. Gradually add the dry ingredients, mixing until combined.
6. Stir in the chocolate chips.
7. Drop rounded tablespoons of dough onto the prepared baking sheets.
8. Bake for 10-12 minutes or until golden brown. Cool on wire racks.

Shortbread Cookies

Ingredients:

- 1 cup unsalted butter, softened
- 1/2 cup granulated sugar
- 2 cups all-purpose flour
- 1/4 tsp salt

Instructions:

1. Preheat the oven to 325°F (165°C) and line a baking sheet with parchment paper.
2. In a large bowl, beat together the butter and sugar until smooth.
3. Gradually add the flour and salt, mixing until a dough forms.
4. Roll the dough out onto a lightly floured surface and cut into shapes with a cookie cutter or slice into rectangles.
5. Place the cookies on the prepared baking sheet and bake for 15-18 minutes, or until the edges are lightly golden.
6. Let the cookies cool on a wire rack.

Caramelized Banana Slices

Ingredients:

- 2 ripe bananas
- 2 tbsp unsalted butter
- 2 tbsp brown sugar
- 1 tsp vanilla extract
- A pinch of cinnamon (optional)

Instructions:

1. Peel the bananas and slice them into 1/2-inch thick rounds.
2. In a skillet, melt the butter over medium heat.
3. Add the brown sugar and stir until it dissolves.
4. Place the banana slices in the skillet and cook for 2-3 minutes per side, until golden and caramelized.
5. Remove from heat and stir in the vanilla extract and cinnamon (if using).
6. Serve warm as a sweet snack or dessert.

Mini Eclairs

Ingredients:

- **For the choux pastry:**
    - 1/2 cup water
    - 1/2 cup unsalted butter
    - 1 cup all-purpose flour
    - 4 large eggs
    - 1/4 tsp salt
- **For the filling:**
    - 1 cup heavy cream
    - 1 tbsp powdered sugar
    - 1 tsp vanilla extract
- **For the glaze:**
    - 1/2 cup semi-sweet chocolate chips
    - 2 tbsp heavy cream

Instructions:

1. Preheat the oven to 400°F (200°C) and line a baking sheet with parchment paper.
2. For the choux pastry, combine water, butter, and salt in a saucepan over medium heat. Once the butter melts, bring to a boil.
3. Remove from heat and stir in the flour until smooth.
4. Let the dough cool for 5 minutes, then add eggs one at a time, mixing well after each addition.
5. Spoon the dough into a piping bag fitted with a round tip. Pipe 3-inch logs onto the baking sheet.
6. Bake for 20-25 minutes until puffed and golden. Let them cool completely.
7. For the filling, whip the heavy cream with powdered sugar and vanilla extract until stiff peaks form.
8. Slice the eclairs in half and pipe the cream filling inside.
9. For the glaze, melt the chocolate and heavy cream in a heatproof bowl over simmering water. Stir until smooth.
10. Dip the top of each eclair in the chocolate glaze and set aside to set. Serve chilled.

Panna Cotta

Ingredients:

- 2 cups heavy cream
- 1 cup whole milk
- 1/2 cup granulated sugar
- 2 tsp vanilla extract
- 2 1/2 tsp powdered gelatin
- 3 tbsp cold water

Instructions:

1. In a small bowl, sprinkle the gelatin over the cold water and let it bloom for 5 minutes.
2. In a saucepan, combine the cream, milk, and sugar. Heat over medium until the sugar dissolves, but do not let it boil.
3. Remove from heat and stir in the vanilla extract.
4. Add the gelatin mixture to the cream mixture, stirring until completely dissolved.
5. Pour the mixture into small serving cups and refrigerate for at least 4 hours or until set.
6. Serve with fresh berries or fruit compote on top.

S'mores Bars

Ingredients:

- 1 1/2 cups graham cracker crumbs
- 1/2 cup unsalted butter, melted
- 1/4 cup granulated sugar
- 2 cups mini marshmallows
- 1 cup milk chocolate chips
- 1/4 tsp vanilla extract

Instructions:

1. Preheat the oven to 350°F (175°C) and line an 8x8-inch baking dish with parchment paper.
2. In a bowl, mix the graham cracker crumbs, melted butter, and sugar until well combined.
3. Press the mixture into the bottom of the prepared baking dish.
4. Bake for 10 minutes, then remove from the oven.
5. Sprinkle the mini marshmallows and chocolate chips on top.
6. Bake for an additional 5-7 minutes, until the marshmallows are golden brown.
7. Let it cool for 30 minutes before cutting into bars. Serve and enjoy!

Frozen Yogurt Bark

Ingredients:

- 2 cups plain Greek yogurt
- 2 tbsp honey or maple syrup
- 1/2 cup mixed berries (strawberries, blueberries, raspberries)
- 1/4 cup granola
- 1/4 cup dark chocolate chips

Instructions:

1. Line a baking sheet with parchment paper.
2. In a bowl, mix the Greek yogurt and honey until smooth.
3. Spread the yogurt mixture evenly onto the prepared baking sheet.
4. Top with berries, granola, and chocolate chips.
5. Freeze for 3-4 hours, or until solid.
6. Break into pieces and serve as a cool, refreshing treat.

Almond Joy Bites

Ingredients:

- 1 cup unsweetened shredded coconut
- 1/4 cup almond butter
- 2 tbsp honey
- 1/2 tsp vanilla extract
- 12 whole almonds
- 1/2 cup dark chocolate chips

Instructions:

1. In a bowl, mix together the coconut, almond butter, honey, and vanilla extract until well combined.
2. Roll the mixture into 12 bite-sized balls.
3. Press an almond into the center of each ball.
4. Melt the dark chocolate chips in the microwave or over a double boiler.
5. Dip each ball into the chocolate and place on a parchment-lined baking sheet.
6. Refrigerate for 30 minutes until the chocolate sets. Serve chilled.

Apple Nachos

Ingredients:

- 2 large apples, thinly sliced
- 1/4 cup peanut butter
- 2 tbsp honey
- 1/4 cup mini chocolate chips
- 1/4 cup crushed nuts (optional)

Instructions:

1. Arrange the apple slices on a large plate or tray.
2. In a microwave-safe bowl, heat the peanut butter and honey together for 20-30 seconds until melted and smooth.
3. Drizzle the peanut butter mixture over the apple slices.
4. Sprinkle with mini chocolate chips and crushed nuts (if using).
5. Serve immediately as a fun, healthy snack or dessert.

Chocolate Covered Bananas

Ingredients:

- 2 ripe bananas
- 1 cup dark or milk chocolate chips
- 1/4 cup crushed nuts or sprinkles (optional)

Instructions:

1. Slice the bananas into 1-inch thick rounds.
2. Melt the chocolate chips in a microwave-safe bowl or over a double boiler until smooth.
3. Dip each banana slice into the melted chocolate, then place on a parchment-lined tray.
4. Sprinkle with crushed nuts or sprinkles if desired.
5. Refrigerate for 30 minutes, or until the chocolate is set. Serve chilled.

Coconut Macaroons

Ingredients:

- 2 1/2 cups unsweetened shredded coconut
- 1/2 cup sweetened condensed milk
- 2 large egg whites
- 1 tsp vanilla extract
- A pinch of salt

Instructions:

1. Preheat the oven to 325°F (163°C) and line a baking sheet with parchment paper.
2. In a large bowl, combine the shredded coconut, sweetened condensed milk, vanilla extract, and salt.
3. In a separate bowl, whisk the egg whites until stiff peaks form.
4. Gently fold the egg whites into the coconut mixture.
5. Using a spoon, scoop rounded portions of the mixture and form small mounds on the prepared baking sheet.
6. Bake for 20-25 minutes, until the macaroons are golden brown.
7. Let them cool before serving.

Strawberry Sorbet

Ingredients:

- 2 cups fresh strawberries, hulled
- 1/2 cup granulated sugar
- 1/2 cup water
- 1 tbsp lemon juice

Instructions:

1. Puree the strawberries in a blender or food processor until smooth.
2. In a small saucepan, combine the sugar and water, and heat over medium heat until the sugar dissolves completely.
3. Let the syrup cool, then stir it into the strawberry puree along with the lemon juice.
4. Pour the mixture into an ice cream maker and churn according to the manufacturer's instructions.
5. Transfer to an airtight container and freeze for 2-3 hours before serving.

Churros

Ingredients:

- 1 cup water
- 2 tbsp unsalted butter
- 1 tbsp granulated sugar
- 1/2 tsp salt
- 1 cup all-purpose flour
- 2 large eggs
- Vegetable oil for frying
- 1/4 cup granulated sugar (for coating)
- 1 tsp ground cinnamon (for coating)

Instructions:

1. In a saucepan, bring water, butter, sugar, and salt to a boil.
2. Remove from heat and stir in the flour until smooth.
3. Let the dough cool for a few minutes, then add the eggs one at a time, mixing well after each addition.
4. Heat vegetable oil in a frying pan over medium heat.
5. Transfer the dough to a piping bag fitted with a star tip. Pipe 6-inch lengths of dough into the hot oil and fry until golden brown, about 2-3 minutes per side.
6. Remove from oil and drain on paper towels.
7. Mix the cinnamon and sugar together, then roll the churros in the mixture.
8. Serve warm.

Key Lime Pie Bites

Ingredients:

- 1 cup graham cracker crumbs
- 1/4 cup melted butter
- 1/4 cup powdered sugar
- 1/2 cup key lime juice
- 1 (8 oz) package cream cheese, softened
- 1/2 cup sweetened condensed milk
- 1/4 cup heavy cream
- Lime zest for garnish (optional)

Instructions:

1. Preheat the oven to 350°F (175°C) and line a mini muffin tin with paper liners.
2. In a bowl, combine the graham cracker crumbs, melted butter, and powdered sugar. Press the mixture into the bottom of each muffin cup to form a crust.
3. Bake the crusts for 5 minutes, then remove from the oven and set aside to cool.
4. In a mixing bowl, beat together the cream cheese, sweetened condensed milk, and key lime juice until smooth.
5. Spoon the filling over the cooled crusts and smooth the tops.
6. Bake for 8-10 minutes, then let cool and refrigerate for at least 2 hours.
7. Garnish with lime zest and serve chilled.

Fruit Popsicles

Ingredients:

- 2 cups fresh fruit (such as berries, mango, or kiwi)
- 1/2 cup coconut water or fruit juice
- 1 tbsp honey or agave syrup (optional)

Instructions:

1. Blend the fresh fruit and coconut water (or juice) in a blender until smooth.
2. Taste the mixture and add honey or agave syrup if desired for extra sweetness.
3. Pour the mixture into popsicle molds.
4. Insert sticks and freeze for at least 4 hours, or until fully frozen.
5. To release the popsicles, run warm water over the outside of the molds for a few seconds.

Brownie Cookies

Ingredients:

- 1 cup semi-sweet chocolate chips
- 1/2 cup unsalted butter
- 1 cup granulated sugar
- 2 large eggs
- 1 tsp vanilla extract
- 1 cup all-purpose flour
- 1/2 tsp baking powder
- A pinch of salt

Instructions:

1. Preheat the oven to 350°F (175°C) and line a baking sheet with parchment paper.
2. In a microwave-safe bowl, melt the chocolate chips and butter together, stirring every 30 seconds until smooth.
3. In a separate bowl, whisk together the sugar, eggs, and vanilla extract until light and fluffy.
4. Fold in the melted chocolate mixture.
5. In another bowl, whisk the flour, baking powder, and salt, then gradually add it to the wet mixture.
6. Drop spoonfuls of the dough onto the prepared baking sheet.
7. Bake for 10-12 minutes, or until the edges are set but the centers are still soft.
8. Let cool on the baking sheet before serving.

Mini Cheesecakes

Ingredients:

- 1 cup graham cracker crumbs
- 1/4 cup melted butter
- 2 tbsp sugar
- 2 (8 oz) packages cream cheese, softened
- 1/2 cup granulated sugar
- 2 large eggs
- 1 tsp vanilla extract
- 1/4 cup sour cream

Instructions:

1. Preheat the oven to 325°F (163°C) and line a muffin tin with paper liners.
2. In a small bowl, mix the graham cracker crumbs, melted butter, and sugar until combined. Press a tablespoon of the mixture into the bottom of each muffin cup.
3. In a large bowl, beat the cream cheese and sugar until smooth. Add eggs one at a time, mixing well after each addition. Stir in the vanilla extract and sour cream.
4. Spoon the cream cheese mixture over the crust in each muffin cup.
5. Bake for 20-25 minutes, or until the centers are set.
6. Let cool to room temperature, then refrigerate for at least 4 hours before serving.

Snickerdoodle Cookies

Ingredients:

- 1 3/4 cups all-purpose flour
- 1 tsp baking soda
- 1/2 tsp cream of tartar
- 1/4 tsp salt
- 1/2 cup unsalted butter, softened
- 1 cup granulated sugar
- 2 large eggs
- 1 tsp vanilla extract
- 2 tbsp granulated sugar (for rolling)
- 1 tsp ground cinnamon (for rolling)

Instructions:

1. Preheat the oven to 350°F (175°C) and line a baking sheet with parchment paper.
2. In a bowl, whisk together the flour, baking soda, cream of tartar, and salt.
3. In another bowl, cream the butter and sugar together until light and fluffy.
4. Add the eggs one at a time, mixing well after each addition, then stir in the vanilla extract.
5. Gradually add the dry ingredients to the wet mixture, mixing until combined.
6. In a small bowl, combine the sugar and cinnamon for rolling.
7. Roll the dough into 1-inch balls and then roll each ball in the cinnamon-sugar mixture.
8. Place on the baking sheet and bake for 8-10 minutes, or until the edges are golden.
9. Let cool on the baking sheet before transferring to a wire rack.

Chocolate Lava Mug Cake

Ingredients:

- 4 tbsp all-purpose flour
- 4 tbsp granulated sugar
- 2 tbsp cocoa powder
- 1/8 tsp baking powder
- A pinch of salt
- 3 tbsp milk
- 2 tbsp vegetable oil
- 1/4 tsp vanilla extract
- 1 tbsp chocolate chips

Instructions:

1. In a microwave-safe mug, whisk together the flour, sugar, cocoa powder, baking powder, and salt.
2. Add the milk, vegetable oil, and vanilla extract, and stir until smooth.
3. Drop the chocolate chips in the center of the batter.
4. Microwave on high for 1 minute and 30 seconds, or until the cake has risen and the center is soft.
5. Let it cool slightly before serving. Enjoy the gooey chocolate center!

Chocolate Peanut Butter Cups

Ingredients:

- 1 1/2 cups semi-sweet chocolate chips
- 1/2 cup creamy peanut butter
- 1/4 cup powdered sugar
- 1/4 tsp vanilla extract
- A pinch of salt

Instructions:

1. Line a muffin tin with paper liners.
2. Melt the chocolate chips in a microwave-safe bowl, stirring every 30 seconds until smooth.
3. In a separate bowl, mix the peanut butter, powdered sugar, vanilla extract, and salt until well combined.
4. Spoon a small amount of melted chocolate into the bottom of each muffin liner, then add a spoonful of the peanut butter mixture.
5. Cover with more melted chocolate and refrigerate for 2 hours, or until firm.
6. Serve chilled or at room temperature.

Pumpkin Spice Muffins

Ingredients:

- 1 3/4 cups all-purpose flour
- 1 tsp baking soda
- 1/2 tsp baking powder
- 1 1/2 tsp ground cinnamon
- 1/2 tsp ground nutmeg
- 1/4 tsp ground ginger
- A pinch of ground cloves
- 1/2 tsp salt
- 1/2 cup vegetable oil
- 1 cup granulated sugar
- 2 large eggs
- 1 cup canned pumpkin puree
- 1 tsp vanilla extract

Instructions:

1. Preheat the oven to 350°F (175°C) and line a muffin tin with paper liners.
2. In a bowl, whisk together the flour, baking soda, baking powder, cinnamon, nutmeg, ginger, cloves, and salt.
3. In another bowl, mix the oil and sugar until combined. Add the eggs, one at a time, and beat well.
4. Stir in the pumpkin puree and vanilla extract.
5. Gradually add the dry ingredients to the wet ingredients and mix until just combined.
6. Divide the batter evenly among the muffin cups.
7. Bake for 20-25 minutes, or until a toothpick inserted into the center comes out clean.
8. Let cool before serving.

Lemon Sorbet

Ingredients:

- 1 1/2 cups fresh lemon juice (about 6 lemons)
- 1 cup water
- 3/4 cup granulated sugar
- Zest of 2 lemons

Instructions:

1. In a small saucepan, combine the water and sugar over medium heat. Stir until the sugar dissolves completely. Remove from heat and let cool.
2. Stir in the lemon juice and lemon zest.
3. Pour the mixture into an ice cream maker and churn according to the manufacturer's instructions.
4. Once churned, transfer the sorbet to an airtight container and freeze for at least 2-3 hours.
5. Serve chilled and enjoy!

No-Bake Oatmeal Cookies

Ingredients:

- 2 cups old-fashioned rolled oats
- 1/2 cup creamy peanut butter
- 1/4 cup unsweetened cocoa powder
- 1/2 cup granulated sugar
- 1/4 cup milk
- 1/2 tsp vanilla extract
- A pinch of salt

Instructions:

1. In a medium saucepan, combine the sugar, cocoa powder, and milk. Bring to a boil over medium heat, stirring frequently.
2. Boil for 1-2 minutes, then remove from heat and stir in the peanut butter, vanilla extract, and salt until smooth.
3. Stir in the rolled oats until well combined.
4. Drop spoonfuls of the mixture onto a parchment-lined baking sheet.
5. Refrigerate for at least 30 minutes, or until set.
6. Enjoy your chewy, no-bake oatmeal cookies!

White Chocolate Raspberry Bark

Ingredients:

- 1 1/2 cups white chocolate chips
- 1/2 cup freeze-dried raspberries, crushed
- 1/4 cup chopped pistachios (optional)
- 1/4 cup raspberry jam (optional for extra flavor)

Instructions:

1. Line a baking sheet with parchment paper.
2. Melt the white chocolate chips in a microwave-safe bowl, stirring every 30 seconds until smooth.
3. Pour the melted white chocolate onto the prepared baking sheet and spread it evenly.
4. Gently swirl in the raspberry jam (if using) for a marbled effect.
5. Sprinkle the crushed freeze-dried raspberries and pistachios over the white chocolate.
6. Refrigerate for at least 1 hour or until set.
7. Break the bark into pieces and enjoy!

Simple Ice Cream Sandwiches

Ingredients:

- 1 batch of cookies (chocolate chip, oatmeal, or your favorite kind)
- 2 cups ice cream (any flavor you like, softened slightly)

Instructions:

1. Bake your cookies according to the recipe and let them cool completely.
2. Scoop a generous amount of softened ice cream onto the bottom of one cookie.
3. Place a second cookie on top and gently press together to form a sandwich.
4. For a firmer texture, wrap the sandwiches in plastic wrap and freeze for 30 minutes before serving.
5. Enjoy these homemade ice cream sandwiches!

Chocolate Coconut Energy Balls

Ingredients:

- 1 cup rolled oats
- 1/4 cup unsweetened cocoa powder
- 1/4 cup shredded coconut
- 2 tbsp honey or maple syrup
- 2 tbsp peanut butter or almond butter
- 1/4 cup mini chocolate chips
- 1/2 tsp vanilla extract

Instructions:

1. In a large bowl, combine the oats, cocoa powder, shredded coconut, chocolate chips, and vanilla extract.
2. Add the peanut butter and honey/maple syrup, mixing everything until well combined.
3. Roll the mixture into small bite-sized balls and place them on a parchment-lined baking sheet.
4. Refrigerate for at least 30 minutes to firm up.
5. Store in an airtight container in the fridge for up to 1 week.

Pineapple Coconut Bites

Ingredients:

- 1 cup dried pineapple, chopped into small pieces
- 1/2 cup shredded coconut
- 1/4 cup honey or maple syrup
- 1/4 tsp vanilla extract

Instructions:

1. In a food processor, combine the chopped pineapple, shredded coconut, honey/maple syrup, and vanilla extract.
2. Pulse until the mixture comes together and sticks together when pressed.
3. Roll the mixture into small balls and place them on a parchment-lined baking sheet.
4. Refrigerate for 30 minutes or until firm.
5. Enjoy these tropical bites!

Jello Parfaits

Ingredients:

- 1 package (3 oz) of flavored gelatin (such as strawberry or lime)
- 1 1/2 cups boiling water
- 1/2 cup cold water
- 1 cup whipped cream or whipped topping
- Fresh fruit for layering (optional, such as berries or kiwi)

Instructions:

1. Dissolve the gelatin in boiling water, stirring until fully dissolved. Add the cold water and refrigerate for 1-2 hours until it begins to set but is not fully firm.
2. Once the gelatin is slightly set, whip the cream or topping until stiff peaks form.
3. In small glass cups or jars, layer the gelatin, whipped cream, and fresh fruit. You can repeat the layers for more texture.
4. Refrigerate the parfaits until fully set, about 4 hours.
5. Serve chilled and enjoy your refreshing treat!

www.ingramcontent.com/pod-product-compliance
Lightning Source LLC
LaVergne TN
LVHW081336060526
838201LV00055B/2681